Help with Hauntings
A Guide to Cleansing your Home
Of Spirits & Ghosts

Dawn Flowers

Tanjia,

Hope this serves you well. Wishing you the best!

— Dawn Flowers

Dearest Reader,

Thank you for your interest in my work, and for giving me an opportunity to help you and your family restore peace in your home. It's my sincerest hope that the information and methods presented here will help you, as it has others. This material is the same information I've given clients who've reached out for help, and the same methods I've used to expel entities from their homes and businesses. It's worked for me, it's worked for others, and I'm confident it can work for you, too.

Though I've worked closely with other investigators and researchers, I'd like to clarify that the opinions and statements expressed within this book are entirely my own and may not reflect the views of my colleagues or groups to which I'm affiliated with or mention within these pages. Each researcher and/or investigator has their own theories and beliefs, which I respect greatly, and so it's not my intention to speak for anyone but myself. These are my theories, beliefs, and practices. Any mistakes or errors found within these pages are also mine.

My intention with this project was to create a concise and economical tool which serves as a quick read for people who need affordable help in a hurry. The personal stories shared are to give a little context to my theories, but even so, I hope I didn't ramble too much, and you're able to quickly find peace and comfort within these pages. I wish you the best of luck, and the brightest of blessings.

~Dawn Flowers

TABLE OF CONTENTS

7	Introduction
11	Should I Investigate?
13	How to Investigate & Equipment Needed?
17	Should I Communicate?
19	How Do I Communicate?
21	Should I Research?
23	How do I Research?
25	Aren't all Spirits Bad?
31	Why do Ghost Linger?
33	Can Hauntings Cause Mental Illness?
35	How Can Spirits Affect Children?
37	What Can I do for my child?
41	Can Spirits Affect Pets?
43	Should I Seek Paranormal Services?
49	Should I Have an Exorcism?
61	Cleansing Prayer Notations
59	Christian Prayers
60	Cleansing (Solo Version)
62	Cleansing (Group Version)
64	Cleansing (Leader's Version)
66	Banishing (Solo Version)
68	Banishing (Group Version)
70	Banishing (Leader's Version)
73	Jewish Prayers
74	Cleansing (Solo Version)
76	Cleansing (Group Version)
78	Cleansing (Leader's Version)
80	Banishing (Solo Version)
82	Banishing (Group Version)
84	Banishing (Leader's Version)

87	Wiccan Prayers
88	Cleansing (Solo Version)
90	Cleansing (Group Version)
92	Cleansing (Leader's Version)
94	Banishing (Solo Version)
96	Banishing (Group Version)
98	Banishing (Leader's Version)
101	Native American Prayers
102	Cleansing (Solo Version)
104	Cleansing (Group Version)
106	Cleansing (Leader's Version)
108	Banishing (Solo Version)
110	Banishing (Group Version)
112	Banishing (Leader's Version)
115	Thank you
117	In Memory of Bob Bowman
119	About Dawn Flowers
120	Other Books
122	Copyright Information

Introduction

Chances are, if you're reading this book, your house is haunted. You're probably upset, nervous, and scared. Understandably, so. Anyone in your situation would be, but you don't have to be. The information presented here will help you maintain a calm, controlled, and active role in removing spirits in your home and de-haunting your house. With this material, you'll have the tools to get rid of the ghosts and gain control of your life.

Conditions inside a haunted house can range from mildly amusing to utterly traumatic. This book was written with severe cases in mind, where injuries are occurring, children are scared, or when the daily fear has become a constant dark cloud hanging over a family. This book was written for people who feel trapped in their homes or trapped by their situation.

Two questions I usually ask clients when I meet with them the first time, are whether they attend a church, and whether they've sought their church's help. I don't like stepping on any spiritual toes in my work, and so if you're religious, then I encourage you to speak first with your spiritual advisor, whether that's a preacher, minister, rabbi, priest, priestess, etc., if you can. This book isn't meant to replace your faith's doctrines or methods. It's meant as a supplemental guide for when your faith's leaders don't or won't help with the haunting, or if you don't have a spiritual group you can reach out to.

I've included several variations of the cleansing prayers to accommodate several religious paths, and a variety of scenarios, since every home and every haunting is different. It's my hope that you'll find one suitable for your needs. If you don't, feel free to modify any version to suit your circumstances. It's the intent behind the prayer, not the wording, that matters, so feel free to make any adjustments to suit your needs.

My first and foremost agenda in writing this book is to promote positive mental, spiritual, and physical health for individuals and families who are suffering from the trauma of living in a haunted house. It's frightening and confusing, and I hope to guide you toward a more positive future for yourself and your loved ones.

If you find yourself in tears every day, it's important that you recognize that it's becoming traumatic, and it's not a healthy environment. I urge you to consider contacting a family therapist. *Not* because I think you're crazy, but because the stress and fear from living in a haunted house can be overwhelming and traumatic, and a therapist can help you and your family work through that trauma.

When people's lives become disrupted after witnessing unexplainable or disturbing events, often they don't know what to do, or what's going to happen next, nor how to stop it from happening again. Unless a person lives in a large city, or a town with at least one paranormal research team, people are often left on their own to seek answers, and solutions can seem intimidating and frightening.

In my younger years, I encountered an entity as a teenager, and again in my early twenties. The events left an impression on me and served as a catalyst for my interests in the paranormal. Years later, when my family moved into our current home, we experienced several other strange occurrences, and those events eventually led to my involvement with Lufkin Paranormal Investigators (LPI), a phenomenal group of guys in the East Texas area that I've been privileged to work with for several years now. I'm fortunate beyond words that LPI founder, Chad Hughes, and his colleague, Tim Smith, welcomed me to join them as they investigate East Texas hauntings. We've each felt, through our work and our own experiences, the same heart-pounding fear that you're likely experiencing right now, and we've come to realize, that there *are* ways to cope, and there is *hope*.

Working with Chad and Tim in the field afforded me the opportunity to meet a beautiful assortment of people, witness numerous strange occurrences, see vast amounts of compelling evidence, and hear the recounting of dozens of experiences. We've gained insights too, into common fears, questions, and concerns that plague haunting victims. Admittedly, I don't have all the answers, but with this simple and easy to understand information, I'll help guide you through the spiritual, physical, and mental aspects of your haunting, and give you the insights you need to perform your own investigations and research, and ultimately stop the haunting.

For the sake of clarity, I'd like to point out the distinctions I make between *investigate* and *research,* as used throughout the course of this book. For our purposes, *investigate* shall refer to the collection of evidence directly related to the haunting, such as witness statements, photos, videos, voice recordings, temperature readings, energy readings, etc. *Research* shall be used to describe the background and historical information concerning the property or the people where the haunting occurred, such as property deeds, obituaries, etc.

Should I Investigate?

You don't *need* evidence before you perform a cleansing on your home or property, and so, investigations aren't *entirely* necessary, *but* they can be immensely rewarding. Gathering information and evidence can be empowering. When you collect data on film or through audio, it can serve as the proof you feel you need, to convince others of your sanity. Evidence can certainly provide people with some validity, but it's not *absolutely necessary* before performing a cleansing prayer.

If you investigate, and subsequently acquire proof, its legitimacy might be questioned by the die-hard skeptics in your life. Spending hundreds of dollars on equipment and research, to impress or convince others should not be your motivating factor for having an investigation. Non-believers will find a way not to believe, and you'll walk away disappointed if they say you faked the footage.

If you're genuinely curious, and simply want to know what might be going on behind the scenes, for *you*, then certainly, I'd recommend spending a little time and money for research and an investigation prior to a cleansing.

Some folks believe that an investigation could stir up activity, and they choose not to engage in any sort of investigative or historical research. Thinking back on the investigations I've participated with, only a small percent of people reported an increase in activity after an investigation. It's not many. Of those, the occurrences dwindled after several cleansings, so even with small bouts of initial increased activity after the investigation, the hauntings were eased over time, so it might be worth it for you. Those are good odds, if you're the gambling type, and your haunting isn't already malicious or physical. I wouldn't recommend stirring up something that was already sinister, even with those odds. In fact, if you feel like you're already in physical danger, I'd recommend that you skip the investigation and postpone any research until after a cleansing.

How to Investigate? What Equipment is Needed?

When investigating homes, our team uses several common devises and several specialized devices to gather data. We take photos, video, and audio recordings using the same devices you might use, including cameras, video recorders, audio recorders, thermometers, and even our phones. In fact, the average smartphone can serve as at least three instruments in one, taking photos, audio, and video recording. Additional apps are available for most smart phones, such as the Ghost Box, or other specialized video and audio apps. Smart phones these days make great investigative tools, for as long as the batteries and memory storage hold out. For lengthy video or audio recordings you'd do well to invest in decent video and audio recorders with larger memory capabilities.

Electromagnetic Field Detectors

Our team also takes energy readings using electromagnetic field detectors. Though specialized, these devises are readily available for purchase on the internet, with some instruments falling well below a hundred dollars, it allows anyone to initiate their own electromagnetic study of their home.

Electromagnetic field detectors come in a variety of styles and prices. For a simple investigation, I'd recommend an inexpensive hand-held model designed specifically for household use. Take the instrument around your home at different times, making note of normal spikes around high-traffic electrical areas, near the breaker box, and near appliances, and electrical wirings within the walls.

Video & Audio Recordings

For your investigation, you might consider setting up a video recorder in your high-traffic haunted areas. If the activity seems concentrated in one area, you might record through the night. As you record, make note of common noises that are heard. Passing cars, wind, air conditioning units, refrigerators, etc. can all make noises which might sound odd to you on the footage as you review it. Make sure you identify and note those noises as they occur, to prevent any confusion when you review the data later. The same applies to lighting sources, such as passing car lights and lighting. If there's a storm in the area, make note of this on the video or audio footage, particularly if you see lightning or hear thunder.

Thermometers

Placing thermometers around the affected areas might also prove helpful, allowing you to record variations in the room's temperature at different spots. Thermometers come in all sizes, shapes, and prices, but if you're on a budget, you can hit up your local dollar shop and get several to place throughout your home. Ideally, during the course of the investigation, you'd want to turn off heating and cooling devices for temperature readings, but this isn't always feasible. In these cases, make note of the air vents as you place your thermometers and avoid the air-flow path around the vents. What I generally look for are obvious and exceptional temperature spikes, which exceed environmental explanation. For example, if it's 60 Fahrenheit outside, and your home's air conditioning unit is set at 70 F, you'd want to look for temperatures below 60 F, and above 70 F. If you have a set of circumstances like that, such as a temperature spike of 80 F, or a drop to 50 F, then you'd want to investigate these variations a bit further to ensure any hot spots weren't natural light or electrically related from appliances. If you can't explain the temperature fluctuations, then you should certainly consider setting up recording devices in that area to monitor for evidence of spiritual activity.

Each of these instruments and their usefulness vary, though. What constitutes as evidence, also varies, depending on the person collecting or reviewing the data. For example, finding orbs on photos is concrete evidence to some, while other investigators ascertain orbs to be dust and insects. I personally don't accept orbs as concrete evidence by themselves, but I've seen a few that gave me chills, so I keep an open mind, but my general rule is to not accept them as concrete evidence alone.

The same logic applies to other forms of evidence, and so there are no clear lines drawn to distinguish what *is* evidence and what *isn't*. Photos, video, and audio can all be easily faked, and so others might see your evidence and immediately shoot it down as fraudulent, and you'll feel like your efforts were in vain, and they were, if your only goal was to convince *others* that your haunting is legitimate. If you choose to research and investigate, do it for *you*, and you won't be disappointed.

Should I Communicate?

Whether or not you should communicate with a spirit depends entirely on your situation and your religious or personal beliefs. It's your call. If you're frightened that it might become agitated and cause increased activity, then don't communicate with it. Skip right to the cleansing. If you do communicate with it, it might be creepy, and you might get a little freaked out, but I don't think communication alone will be enough to cause an explosion of activity, at least from what I've seen. If you're curious, I'd give it a go. If you're frightened, I'd take a pass.

Considerations might also be made depending on your religious or spiritual path. Some paths frown on communications with spirits. While the Old and New Testaments acknowledge spirits, demons, and ghosts, they also clearly condemn attempts to interact or communicate with them. If you're Jewish, I'd take a pass on trying to communicate with the spirits, so as not to act against advice from the Torah regarding spiritualism. For Christians, it depends on the denomination, but it's generally frowned upon to engage with spirits. Most widely respected doctrines advise against what I call, *meddling*, which involves any sort of back and forth dealings, such as asking questions, either through a séance, a Ouija board, an EVP session, etc. There seems to be more wiggle room with regard to Spiritualism amongst offshoots of Christianity, and so how far you meddle depends on you and your path.

If you decide to meddle a little and try to communicate with a spirit, just keep in mind there are a ton of religious texts that advise against it. The general consensus is that spirits are notoriously deceptive and can engage in trickery and lying. So, be careful when engaging with Ouija boards, séances, or during EVP session. As long as you're aware that the potential for deception is there, it goes a long way toward helping you decipher the credibility of the spirit you communicate with.

When you try to interact with a spirit, beyond telling it to leave, then you raise your risk of encountering an entity with evil intentions, but I don't think they've *all* got evil intentions, a subject I'll touch on in a few moments. But, if you're engaging with an entity that you *know* is trying to scare the hell outta everyone in the house, then you should probably remain leery of any information obtained through your communications with it. I wouldn't trust anything or anyone that comes across as intimidating, hostile, or frightening.

How Do I Communicate?

If you're interested, there are several devices used to promote communications with spirits. As with most things though, their legitimacy or illegitimacy are arguable. Personally, I view ouija boards, ghost boxes, séances, and recording devices as tools that make it easier for spirits to communicate with us, and it makes it easier for us to receive it. I don't view these tools as doorways or portals, and I don't believe they open-up anything that wasn't already opened. I perceive these tools as amplifiers in a way, sort of like a megaphone. Whether or not they work rests entirely on the spirit, in my opinion. I feel if a spirit wants to communicate, it'll use whatever is available, whether that's a Ouija board or by slamming the doors on the kitchen cabinet. If you provide the appropriate tools, you might see less broken dishes.

Electronic Voice Phenomena (EVP)

One of the easiest ways to receive possible communications are through EVP's (Electronic Voice Phenomena). Simply set up a voice or video recorder and record the environment. Asking questions to illicit answers is the most common method, and typically these spiritual Q&A's are called *EVP Sessions*. When recording, whether its video or audio, its important to be as quiet as possible. When you review the recordings later, any electronic voice phenomenon will be easier to recognize if other noises are limited. It's also helpful to make an audible note while you're recording to indicate any noises made by those present.

If there are dogs barking in the distance, you should mention that on the audio recording. If someone coughs, you should mention that, too, so that you and others will know immediately what the noises are as the recordings are reviewed.

Should I Research?

The same necessities, or lack of, apply for research as they do for an investigation. It's not *required*, but it might prove rewarding for you to research the property or previous occupants. Insights might develop as you dig, and you might find a name or two behind your trouble. Should you decide to communicate, having an identity and a name to direct your questions toward might prove helpful.

Be warned, your lackadaisical research can turn less-lackadaisical and more *daunting*, the deeper you delve, but the information has the potential to reveal interesting and compelling insights. I recently researched a lone grave that rested near my neighborhood, and in so doing, found an explanation behind her isolated burial. She was Native American and died during a time when the burial of natives was prohibited within the town's Christian cemetery. As a child, I'd visited her grave, which sat in a little patch of woods that the neighborhood kids called, *The Big Woods*. I helped keep the brambles and vines from overtaking the obelisk shaped headstone. Several years ago, I went to check on the grave and it was gone. My sister found a new headstone with her name on it at the Ryan's Chapel Cemetery, where she now rests in peace with the other townsfolk. I wouldn't have solved any of my riddles, had it not been for the research I'd done using various ancestry websites, which incidentally also make invaluable tools for researching haunted houses.

My mother and I both perform genetic and ancestral research for our families, and the rabbit holes we jump through are fascinating. Researching homes and properties, haunted or not, is an easy way to travel through time and bring the past alive again, and in many cases, the dead are brought back, too. Not literally, of course, but by researching the deceased, those individuals are being noted, remembered, thought of, and you've made them relevant again. Some researchers and investigators theorize that these notes and nods to the deceased are enough to bring peace to a haunted home. Maybe that's true.

How do I Research?

There are a gazillion different websites and apps to research people these days, but since we're dealing with the deceased, my first stop when needing information about prior occupants is Ancestry.com. I'm not being paid to say that, either. Some consider their subscription fees pricey, but they're worth every penny if you're at a loss and need somewhere to get started. They've got lots of search options for public records and newspapers, and you're likely to stumble upon a relative of the person you're researching. You can view family trees and browse through birth, marriage, and death records. You can also peruse the family's insightful notes, pictures, and articles. It's truly a treasure trove of historical information. Violent deaths, which many believe promote spirits to linger, are often noted and saved to family trees, so Ancestry is certainly worth a look if you're interested in rooting out the cause of your haunting.

Knowing the history and prior occupants might give you a deeper understanding of why this haunting is occurring, but as with investigating, researching isn't necessary before you perform the cleansing prayer. If you're frightened, skip the research and perform the cleansing prayer.

If you're interested in employing researchers or investigators and want exhaustive historical research performed, you'll likely be charged search fees associated with the research. Most paranormal researchers are generous to the point of not charging for their time, or the use of their equipment, or for the evaluation of the data, and so if they charge small search fees to cover their research dues, you're getting a pretty good deal. Some investigators might also charge for USB sticks or CD's with collected data and evidence, which again, is usually only to recoup their out of pocket cost, and not their time. Small fees are normal, regardless of the extent of the investigation, if goods are provided at the end.

Many paranormal researchers and investigators are able to perform free or low-cost basic research and in-home investigations by utilizing free public documents and electronically sending the collected data and evidence to the clients. It depends entirely on the desires of the home or business owner as to how far the research goes, and the same applies to you, as you decide how much time and money you want to spend on the historical research.

Aren't all Spirits Bad?

According to several respected religious texts, yes, but I respectfully disagree. I don't believe all spirits are bad. I think some of them certainly are, but I firmly believe that a spirit's disposition will be in the afterlife, just as it was in life.

I mentioned earlier that my mother and I do a bit of genealogy and ancestral research, and we've come to realize that it's important to keep our ancestors relevant, whether that's through stories, an incredible cake recipe, or going to events honoring those that have long passed. On one such trip to honor the fallen men at the Alamo in San Antonio, I had a brief moment with what I believe might have been a sweet and kind spirit.

We'd been in town honoring our beloved Jesse B. Bowman, my fourth great-grandfather, who bravely perished during the famous battle on March 6th, 1836. After attending the memorial service at the Alamo, we walked back to our rooms at The Menger Hotel, right across the street. Much later that evening, nearing two in the morning, I snuck downstairs for a cigarette before retiring for the night. When I walked outside through the automatic double doors, the biting cold slapped me in the face. I parked myself on a bench near the valet station, a few yards from the entrance. I lit my cigarette and being unprepared for the cold night, I started shivering. I was dedicated, though. I sat on that bench and stared at the Alamo wall directly in front of me, intent to finish my cigarette. There were no people to distract from the cold. I'd not seen a soul since I left my room, and there was no traffic to watch on the street between me and the Alamo. Everything was dead quiet, so I sat there and watched the wall and shivered. That is, until I heard the distinct sound of the automatic doors sliding open and huge wave a warm wind from the hotel lobby enveloped me. Then I wasn't cold anymore. I was warm and a bit surprised to find no one standing in the doorway.

I waited a moment longer, and still, no one appeared. After a few long seconds the doors closed on their own. The ordeal warmed me up enough to finish my cigarette. I sat there for a minute wondering if I'd been visited by a helpful spirit. Had there been a car or two on the road, I might've assumed that the vibrations from a passing car activated the doors, but there were no cars, either. Mechanical glitch? Or, a helpful spirit? I can't say for sure, but with all the spirits roaming around San Antonio, which is considered one of the most haunted towns in Texas, it's not beyond the realm of reason to assume a few of them might be helpful enough to warm up a chilled lady, and I've even wondered since if it might've even been our beloved Jessie B. Bowman.

I've wondered also if a spirit didn't have a hand in helping save my son's life when he was an infant. It was late at night, he and I were both asleep. He was in his crib and I'd fallen asleep a few feet away while wearing headphones and watching a movie. I'm hard of hearing, and I'd put them on so the noise from the television wouldn't wake him.

I don't know what woke me up, or how I knew, but I woke up in a panic knowing that my son was in trouble. I jumped up and looked in the crib and he was cocooned inside a twisted blanket, head and all. He wasn't crying or hollering, just writhing around trying to get free from the cocoon. The blanket was twisted so tightly around his face, I had to pull him out of the crib to untangle him. Between being hard of hearing and having the headphones on, I don't think I'd heard him cry out. I'm almost convinced that one of my grandmothers woke me up.

So, to answer the question posed: *Aren't all spirits bad?* I've gotta say, *nah*.

Though, this really depends on your personal religious beliefs, as Christian and Jewish texts indicate that spirits can be deceptive, engaging in trickery, can't be trusted and communications or meddling with them should be avoided and are condemnable as acts of Witchcraft and sorcery. One person's meddling is another person's sin, it seems.

Now, as an eclectic follower of several faiths, I've had to sort through all these different philosophies and pull together the most reasonable assumptions from each of these paths to find a truth that speaks to me, with regard to my personal experiences. In so doing, I don't think every entity is evil, but I also don't think they're all *nice* either. Like the living, they go both ways, as dispositions are apt to do.

So, before you cleanse your home, you might consider taking a moment to reflect on whether the spirit is *actually* a negative entity. But, if you're frightened or if you have frightened children in the home, perform the cleansing prayer without hesitations, and certainly without guilt. You and your child's safety and general well-being trumps the spiritual activity, regardless of the spirit's disposition, in my opinion.

One night, many years ago, while avoiding my husband's snoring, I'd crashed on the couch in our play room with my old tom cat, Ginger Boy. I can't say exactly *what* woke me up that night either, but when I found myself awake, I noticed an odd hum. I could hear it and *feel* it. I was curled up on the couch facing the back, with my back to the room. When I opened my eyes, I could see two things from my position, the back of the couch, and the space around it being illuminated in a red-orange glow. Ginger Boy, positioned on the arm of the couch directly behind my head, was growling at something in the middle of the playroom, presumably at the source of the red-orange glow.

Every single one of my internal alarm-bells went off and I knew there was someone or something behind me. My cat's growls and hisses were angry and directed at *something*. I also knew in that moment that if I rolled over to see it, that I wouldn't be able to *unsee* it. My alarm bells were telling me, d*on't do it*. Without turning around, I reached up and laid my hand on Ginger Boy's back to calm him. I could feel that he was crouched in pounce-mode. He stopped growling for a second and that's when I realized that the hum I was hearing, *was not him.* It sounded *electric,* whatever it was, and I presumed that it too came from whatever or whoever was in the center of the playroom.

I've never felt such a strong urge to *not* do something, as I did in that moment, and so I laid there knowing through every fiber of my being that I should *not* turn around. And so, with my face toward the back of the couch and through barely opened eyes, I looked at the red-orange wall behind the couch, and an Ancient Egyptian inspired painting that hung on it, also illuminated in the red-orange glow.

Ginger Boy resumed hissing and growling, and I watched the red-orange wall. I could still *feel* the hum. While my brain scrambled to make sense of the hum, the light, and the angry cat, I wanted to look, but but my gut was still screaming. *Do not look. Wait.*

Everything about this moment was bizarre, and for a moment I thought I might've been dreaming, or having a nightmare. No such luck. That kind of panic within a dream would have *absolutely* woken me up. I followed my instincts. I laid there with my hand on Ginger Boy, and we waited. Several seconds passed and my cat relaxed his posture and stopped hissing and growling. Then, the red-orange glow disappeared, followed by the hum, and all was back to normal.

By this time, my heart was pounding, and my eyes were wide open. I knew the ordeal was over, and that it had *not* been a dream. I knew all was well again. I turned around knowing it was safe and saw exactly what I'd hoped. Nothing. Sometimes, not knowing is better, even if it leaves unanswered questions.

Was it a spirit or maybe a demon of some sort? Perhaps. I honestly couldn't say. All I *can* say for sure is that it was *evil*, and it was *wrong*, which is what my gut was screaming at the time. Was it a burglar with a red tinted light and a vehicle outside making the humming noise? Was it red ball-lightening lingering in my playroom? Was it aliens? Your guess is as good as mine, but it was damn scary. I'm also pretty confident its disposition wasn't good.

So, while some entities are helpful, some are not, leaving me to believe that there is *some* truth and necessity in the religious texts that advise against interacting with spirits. It's certainly a gamble when you choose to communicate with entities, so be careful, my friend.

Why do Ghost Linger?

As noted previously, some folks believe that violent deaths cause spirits to linger, but for the rest of them, truthfully, I don't have a formal or even a generic answer that will fit all circumstances, but I'd imagine that spirits linger in death for the same reasons people linger in life. Whether for love, money, or even madness, our motives in life can be simple or complex, obvious or secretive, and this same logic (or absence of it) can be applied to spirits.

Admittedly, the complexities of their consciousness are beyond my understanding, and so I'm not at liberty to say exactly what makes them tick, or why they linger in one spot, any more than I'm capable of telling you why my neighbors are lingering next door. Though if I had to guess, I'd say my neighbors live where they live because of familiarity and family. Most of my neighbors were born and raised in our town, and when they bought houses, they bought them here because that's where their families were. Some folks moved on, certainly, but the ones that linger...they're here because of an association with the area. There's a familiarity. Or, lower crime rates and cheap real-estate. I'll take a guess and hypothesize that spirits probably aren't concerned about burglary statistics or mortgage points, so, I'd have to guess, they linger where they do, because that's what they know.

The same logic might arguably be applied to cemetery hauntings. I think of graveyards as being like coffee shops. They serve as a predetermined meeting spot where both the living and deceased can gather. I believe that if a person dies, and they know beforehand that their relatives will mourn them with regular visits to their grave, then it might encourage spiritual activity at the cemetery.

The only way to root out a spirit's possible motives, though, is through research, and you'll find that each spirit has an intricate and unique story, as we all do.

Can Hauntings Cause Mental Illness?

In my opinion, that depends on a few factors. If an individual already possesses a psychiatric or psychological condition, then I think it's reasonable to assume that a haunting in the mix wouldn't help their situation, and I can easily see where such circumstances might exacerbate their symptoms, possibly making the existing condition worse. A haunting could certainly serve as a trigger, for those triggered. But…I don't believe the average individual can be made ill, or as some might put it, *driven insane,* by a spirit alone.

If you're dealing with psychologically healthy and psychiatrically fit family members, then I wouldn't consider this a concern. Even with mentally ill or disabled family members, it doesn't mean that they are any more susceptible than others, rather, the haunting might be more confusing for them depending on their condition, but I don't think they are any more at risk than others for being a target.

My youngest son is on the autism spectrum. He swears to this day that he saw a ghost peering in at him with glowing red eyes from outside of our glass door. I tried to reassure him that it was probably a racoon, a possum, or any of the creatures that frequent our porch, but he'd have none of it. He said it was a ghost, with conviction. He's only mentioned one other occurrence, and I doubt he remembers the other incident, which I'll explain more about in a few pages, but otherwise he's a well-adjusted little guy, and I don't think the ordeals exacerbated any of his personal quirks at all, but that's not to say that will be true for all others.

Some children will need more reassurances before they regain their composure. I was fortunate in that he didn't dwell or lose sleep over the "glowing eyes incident" and seemed otherwise unbothered by it, except when it occurred. I don't feel he was targeted or singled out at all. If he truly saw an entity, and not the eyes of a raccoon, I think it was a matter of being in the wrong place at the wrong time. Most of the unusual activity in our home involved the adult family members, so again, I don't believe his Autism was relevant to the events, nor was he a target. I also don't feel that his condition was made worse by the incident, either.

I can only imagine that a similar truth would hold true for others. Drawing from my own experiences at home and in the field, I don't feel that mental issues pull spirits in, or serve as any kind of target for them to hone in on, though as with everything, I'm sure there are exceptions.

I've seen a few wildly hysterical homeowners in the field, which isn't uncommon considering their circumstances, though one or two may or may not have suffered from a panic disorder. Though I'm not qualified to make that determination, I *can* tell you that a haunting in their mix was *not helpful*, and the constant screaming, crying, and high energy antics weren't helpful to the households, either. In that regard, hauntings can certainly add fuel to the fire if there is a panic-driven individual in the home.

How Can Spirits Affect Children?

When hauntings occur, it can be a frightening experience for anyone, but it can be a particularly terrifying ordeal for children. When children are involved in a residential haunting, it's very important, above all else, to help the child believe the home to be safe, *even if you don't believe it yourself.*

Even if the child never experiences any aspect of the haunting itself, panicked parents can send alarm bells to the children in the home, even if they never see or hear a thing. If caretakers speak of the haunting, are physically upset by the haunting, and exhibit otherwise distressing behavior in front of children, they will suffer the same fear, as though they've experienced it themselves. Children are notoriously empathetic, so take care that *you* aren't scaring the child, as the haunting is scaring you.

Some folks believe that children's minds are like blank-slates, more open, free of preconceived notions, void of biases that we form as we age, which impacts one's beliefs and their openness to see spirits as adults. This openness to information, it is said, can serve to draw in spirits like a magnet, making occurrence between the spirit world and children more common. Often times, it's the children who first make note of a haunting in the home, and I believe it's because they're simply more receptive.

There are a variety of theories pertaining to children and hauntings, particularly those where only the children are privy to the spirits. Some of these are going to be imaginary friends, but sadly, some are ghosts, and even sadder, some of these cases demonstrate the early onset of schizophrenia or other mental conditions. It's important for you to educate yourself with the symptoms of schizophrenia so you can recognize any indications. I can't urge you enough to listen to your child, and if you think for a moment that your child might have a condition, then you need to seek appropriate health care, immediately, if you've not done so already.

Unfortunately, the line between mental illness and hauntings can be extremely thin and hard to distinguish. Obviously, if others in the home are experiencing aspects of the haunting as well, then you know its not likely a mental condition by any one person, and you can proceed with investigating, researching, and cleansing the property.

What Can I Do for my Child?

My goal when dealing with children in a haunted home, above all else, is to promote beneficial psychological health, and the best way to do that, is to do whatever is in your means to reassure the child of their safety. In most cases, all that's required for this to happen, is that you calm yourself down, first.

In some cases, parents might not recognize the extent that their own emotions were bleeding onto their children. They're so frightened themselves, they weren't concerned about their children's fears. While this is understandable, once it's recognized, it needs to be addressed and corrected through future behaviors. Plainly put, and I do apologize, but *you've got to get your shit together.* Lucky for you, I can help with that.

You should answer any questions the child may have about the haunting, in a way that is calming and reassuring that the child is safe and will not come to harm. You do not want to excite the child further, and you want to minimize discussions about the haunting when the child is present. The less they know, the better. Truly. But as I said before, answer their questions without causing further alarm.

If you believe the child to be a target within the haunting, and for whatever reason, you can't up and move, its imperative that you work toward keeping your child safe. If the child is being terrorized at night, you might install security cameras to witness your child's behavior prior to, during, and after any spiritual attacks. You might catch a ghost, or you might realize they're experiencing night terrors, which often manifest as vicious nightmares. These realistic dreams often involve imagined monsters of various kinds, including spirits. Video of the child's sleep habits during the night should give you some indication if your child has a sleep disorder, or if there is indeed a targeted haunting. If you believe your child might suffer from night terrors or any sort of sleep disorder, I urge you to speak with your family doctor about the issue. Undiagnosed sleep issues can affect your child's physical and psychological well-being, so I can't beg you enough to root out the cause of your child's nighttime distress, and address it, whether that involves a visit to the doctor or a cleansing.

If you're confident the issues aren't related to a sleep or mental disorder, and you believe the child to be the victim of repeated attacks by a spirit, then I can't urge you enough to listen to your child, and perform a cleansing prayer throughout your home, ASAP.

When they come to you with information about encounters or events, pay close attention to them, and note the details, as these details can give vital information about the nature of the haunting, but otherwise, don't forcefully interrogate the child in a panic. I'd down-play the events as much as possible to the child, then I'd discreetly research and investigate the hell out of it, later. I'm not advocating that you dismiss their fears or lie to them, but rather, maintain a calm and confident attitude that everything will be okay, that you've got this. Because, you do.

Children take their social ques from their parents and caretakers, and if the adults in the house exhibit wildly panicked and frantic behavior, the children will feed off these emotions and will in turn become wildly panicked and frantic themselves. Remember, it is your parental obligation to maintain calm and order, and to make the child feel safe and happy in their home.

Luckily, most parents get it, and they'll do whatever they can to make their child feel safe. In fact, that's why *most* people contact us. They don't want their children to be scared, and so they're receptive to ideas that might help ease their child's trauma. In some of these cases, I've given parents stuffed animals that wore protective crosses. If you have a child that you need to calm, you might try a similar approach. Convey to your child that the stuffed animal's necklace is protective and sleeping with the animal will prevent any harm from coming to the child during the night. As the child grows, they can remove the protective pendant and attach it to an appropriately sized necklace for themselves.

Protective pendants need to reflect your family's religious background, as now is not the time to mix things up, which might be confusing to your child. If you're a Christian, obviously you might consider using a cross, or a charm representing Jesus, Mary, or a Saint. If you're Jewish, then you'd obviously consider a Judaic representation, such as the Star of David. And, if you're Pagan, or Neo Pagan, you might consider a pentacle or any number of God and Goddess representations. If your child was raised

Christian, and you think a protective pentagram is what they need, it's not. Introducing new or strange religious elements will only incite further confusion and fear within the child. Stick with the religion that the child is familiar with, and your efforts at calming your child will be more fruitful.

Can Spirits Affect Pets?

Many people report dogs and cats exhibiting bizarre behavior during hauntings, but these curious behaviors may also extend to birds, horses, pigs, cattle, goats, etc. Most people with pets or livestock that suffer hauntings on their property will report unusual activity from many, if not *all* of their animals, not just the dog.

I've had several experiences myself which come to mind. Recalling one incident in particular, I was sitting at my computer when my youngest son and my dog saw something I didn't. My son (a one-year-old toddler at the time) sat playing with his trains on the floor, when he became extremely upset. He jumped up, ran to me and crawled in my lap, then pointed at *something* in the corner of the room. He cried and hugged me, wanting me to do something about it. My dog, a fearless Chihuahua, at the exact same time, jumped up, ran under my chair, obviously cowering from *something* in the corner of the room, too. My son cried and pointed, while my dog barked and growled, both extremely upset about *something* in the room. I felt extremely helpless and at a loss to calm either one of them, and was about to usher them into the other room when things started to settle down. The ordeal only lasted a few seconds and was over as quickly as it began. My dog stopped growling and came out from under my chair as my son crawled down from my lap and went back to playing with his trains. I still wonder what they saw, and I still have no idea, but I was left convinced that they saw or heard something that I didn't. I also wish I'd had a surveillance in the room that day, on the off chance that something might've showed up.

If you have a pet or own livestock that's exhibiting strange behavior and you've ruled out illnesses that would manifest with similar symptoms, it would absolutely be worth investigating with video surveillance. The ghost in the yard could really be a fox, or what you thought was a fox-might really be a ghost. In any case, you can't go wrong with a surveillance system to help root out the source of your trouble.

Should I Seek Services?

If you feel overwhelmed by the haunting, you might want to seek out a team for help. Often, these teams have seen and heard similar reports and they can be incredibly reassuring and helpful in sharing their insights. Most teams I've worked with are intense networkers and if there's help to be had, they give it, many of them for free. Paranormal researchers are known for being a generous and helpful bunch. For the most part...

There are *some* out there who love nothing more than inciting fear and panic into a household. Most self-respecting investigators, researchers, and cleansers work to keep the drama to a minimum, since they truly care about the psychological health and general well-being of the family and its children. Anyone who goes into a household to perform investigations or cleansings should have a basic understanding of psychology, certainly enough to know that it's not healthy to add fuel to a fire, so to speak, and to tread very lightly when dealing with children.

I would certainly be suspicious of an investigator or cleanser who appears eager to cause additional fright to an already frightened household, and if this occurs, it should serve as a red flag for fraud, since their intentions are usually theatrically motivated, or money driven. Even if they aren't charging a dime, they're getting paid in drama. Everyone has a different motive for being in your home, and you need to understand their motives, in order to determine whether or not their involvement will be helpful or harmful.

I've studied various aspects of the paranormal for the better part of twenty years, and I'm no closer to knowing anything definitive now, than I was *thirty* years ago, except that my theories have evolved, and I'm more confident in some theories than others. This doesn't mean I'm right. I perform investigations and cleansings because I want to learn all I can, and help people regain control in their lives. I want to help people be happier in their daily lives and help them not have negativity looming over their heads. This doesn't make me an expert, it just makes me helpful. Some investigators though, are not so helpful, and their theories are nothing more than fuel for drama, changing the demon per situation to create a high energy situation. Thankfully, these guys are few and far between, and most folks are genuine with their desire to help.

A few clients, and even novice investigators, sometimes expect investigations to proceed quickly, and are often irritated when they don't. If you're dealing with a group of paranormal investigators, be patient. A paranormal investigation can take several weeks from start to finish, and in some cases, studies of the collected data may extend for several months.

I'd also be cautious of anyone willing to pop over to your home in the middle of the night, five minutes after they receive your email, text, instant message, or phone call. If you are frightened to the point that you think you might need help in the middle of the night, it's probably best if you vacate the property until morning, or until you feel it is safe again. Most investigators and research teams don't have people on staff who perform cleansing prayers. The work they do is primarily data collection, in the hopes of collecting evidence for their clients. There *are* teams with people willing to perform cleansings, but they are a minority, and so pleading to your local paranormal investigators to send someone over in the middle of the night probably won't help to stop the haunting, even if they're able to show up.

We've received messages and calls from scared, bleeding, or otherwise traumatized individuals at all hours, nearly every week, sometimes several times a week, and like most groups, we aren't able to respond with a house call in the middle of the night. Most investigators have families and most have other jobs that must be taken into consideration. Patience is the key with most groups, and so I hope you'll take these obligations into consideration when approaching your local group for assistance. And, even still, they might choose not to help you, for whatever reason. Some groups are particular about what they will get involved with, and what they won't. For example, some groups won't take cases that involve suspected possessions. They might feel the problems are beyond their abilities to cope with, and instead might recommend that you approach the Catholic Church for assistance. Some groups might be swamped and overwhelmed with requests for help, and so again, patience is the key in a finding a group that can help.

There are other considerations, too. Most groups like to have their equipment in top-notch shape before arriving on scene. This might include putting fresh batteries in all the investigative equipment. Memory cards need to be checked, uploaded, and cleaned, and made ready for fresh recordings. I can say with some authority that all of this takes a bit of time.

Some groups take some time to run background checks on homeowners or run predator checks on the neighborhood's they're investigating. This might seem excessive to some, but it's not an unreasonable practice. If a lone investigator or a small team is approached by someone who wants them to hang out in their home for a few hours, it helps to know if they've got a violent record before loading up the gear.

Researchers may also request a week or two for historical research on the neighborhood and town before making a visit. Ancestral research on the previous residents can take days, but it's very rewarding. Some researchers prefer to have their ducks in a row, so to speak, before they'll come out to your home, which again, is reasonable.

Between the investigator's family, job, equipment prepping, the residential and ancestral research, the predator checks, and the gathering of team members, you can probably see why they might not be able to help you at 2am. Being patient and respectful, though, will go a long way to finding a helpful team.

Should I Have an Exorcism?

I've had a handful of people reach out to me concerning exorcisms, which is not something I'm willing to perform without a medical professional on hand, and only after the client has undergone a psychiatric evaluation and brain scan. This isn't to suggest that these individuals suffer from a mental malady, rather, it's a precaution used to rule that out.

Possessions exhibit many of the same behaviors and symptoms seen with several psychotic disorders, like schizophrenia and paraphrenia. Some psychotic disorders can be triggered by brain tumors, and so to make sure the individual is truly being helped, it needs to be determined that the individual is physically and mentally healthy before anything is tackled spiritually.

I'm all about the triad: Mind, body, and spirit. Ideally, they work in harmony, but when they don't, it can sometimes be difficult to pinpoint where the disharmony lies: mental, physical, or spiritual. With possessions and their symptomatic similarities to both physical and mental conditions, it's important to look into all possibilities, so the issues, if any exist, can be treated, whether that's through an exorcism, a tumor removal surgery, or a prescription for anti-psychotics. Each of the three are as relevant and important as the others.

If you believe you are possessed, I can't urge you enough to get yourself checked out physically and mentally *before* you seek spiritual help. If you seek spiritual help and find someone willing to perform an exorcism, and they don't insist on medical confirmation that you are mentally and physically healthy before proceeding, your health and well being are *not* their primary concern. Their motivations might vary, but concern for your physical or mental health isn't one of them, and your spiritual health probably isn't *really* one either. In fact, it would make me suspicious of their motives to provide spiritual help. It's hard to imagine there are people concerned enough about one's spiritual health to perform an exorcism, but not enough about their physical or mental health to suggest they get checked out medically before-hand, but they're out there, in many shapes and sizes, and in almost all denominations.

If you think you know someone who you believe is possessed, and you don't encourage them to get tested for health issues, and you forcibly take them to a church or "preacher" to have an exorcism performed, you are not helping the individual. I mention this, because I've seen this scenario play out in my neck of the religious woods. In the Southern US, there are *many* churches and lone practitioners of what I like to call Christian-Craft. These are Christian folks who also participate in rituals to manipulate circumstances or people through acts outside of normal Christian prayer. For example, these folks might engage in exorcism rituals that differ greatly from those held under the respected authority of the Catholic Church. Christian-Crafters will use portions of the Bible to justify whatever their motives are, but with heavy doses of superstition and strong beliefs in the ability of others to curse, or to be cursed. Many use charms, and some might ascribe unnatural powers to objects or people. They believe in witches, though many do not consider themselves as such, and per Biblical scripture, view Witchcraft as evil, despite practicing textbook examples of it themselves.

These folks are found in almost all denominations, everywhere. Generally, their beliefs are an innocent blending of Christianity and Judaism with hints of Voodoo, Witchcraft, and various Native American beliefs mixed in. A melting pot of ideas with the potential to brew up a delicious stew or a rancid poison. Most people who practice this Christian-Craft do so with the most honorable of intentions. I'd be lying if I said I didn't dabble myself a good bit. Most decent folks do and don't realize it. A good-luck charm here and there. There are *some* though, whose motives can quickly turn dark, particularly when it comes to exorcisms.

I've got two close friends who were kidnapped by their families and taken to preachers for an emergency *exorcism*. In both cases, the affected individuals were young adults, and the exorcisms were performed and organized by their parents and their parent's church officials. In both cases, the affected individuals were dating someone their parents didn't like or approve of, and it was determined by the church officials in both cases that the devil was at work, and he could be exorcised out. I think it's also important to understand that these two cases occurred at two different churches, two decades apart, but in the same county. From that, we can only imagine there are a *lot* more stories out there of others who've experienced similar ordeals.

These preachers were not leaders in large churches. Both had congregations that comprised of less than a hundred folks. Their ministerial potency upon their small congregations was strong, nonetheless. They hold high energy exorcisms regularly and the various evil afflictions vary from week to week, depending on the person in need of the exorcism. These afflictions can include any and everything, but regularly include illnesses, possessions of evil spirits, homosexuality, and my personal favorite, when the Devil is making someone date the wrong person.

I'm all for exercising the illness out of someone, if that person is willing, but an unwilling participate in *any* exorcism is wrong. It borders on abuse depending on the way it's carried out. You cannot exercise homosexuality out of someone, either. It's who they are, and it's the way God made them. In my opinion, if one doesn't respect *that*, then they don't have any business speaking, preaching, teaching, or exorcizing in the name of a God they obviously don't respect.

If a preacher seeks to constantly break you down emotionally and spiritually, makes you feel unhappy all the time, or encourages you to be unkind or unaccepting to others, or leaves you feeling without peace about certain issues, then you might want to consider a different preacher. Not all preachers are created equally, and it can sometimes be hard to decipher the good from the bad. If a spiritual leader or advisor constantly makes you feel guilty, sinful, sad, or otherwise causes you to feel badly all the time, then you should probably look for another person or church for guidance, because that's a cult, my friend. If the sermons or advice are a constant stream of emotional manipulation, and the end result is you feeling shitty, its only going to get shittier. If you're getting exercised because they don't like who you're dating, you should really start planning your exit strategy.

I've seen church videos of large groups of children being made to cry over other people's abortions. There were a lot of videos. It's a regular practice for some churches to round the kids up and make them cry every week. Let me be crystal clear here, rounding kids up and making them cry for hours every week isn't spiritual guidance. It's manipulative emotional abuse. It doesn't matter what the content concerns either, whether it's drugs, texting and driving, sex, abortions, being saved, or not being saved. etc. There are more humane ways of conveying the same information to children without inducing a psychological condition. Deliberately depressing children, particularly adolescents who might already suffer from normal teen anxieties is potentially damaging and traumatic. And, I don't think Jesus would be down with that crap. You know those paintings and drawings of Jesus as he's sits talking with children? Note that none of the children are crying.

Thankfully, most religious leaders work with relevant texts and uplifting messages. They preach with the spirit in mind, not outdated agendas. Most leaders focus on the beneficial teachings and their motives are pure. Their goals are usually to help their congregations attain a closer relationship with God and to have peace and happiness in their lives.

Listen to the message, and if that message is based on kindness to yourself and others, peace for yourself and others, and happiness for yourself and others, then it's Godly. Jesus put it best, though, in Mathew 7:12, of the King James Version of the Bible. "Therefore all things whatsoever ye would that men should do to you, do ye even so to them: for this is the law and the prophets." Though, I prefer this translation from the J.B. Phillips New Testament, "Treat other people exactly as you would like to be treated by them - this is the essence of all true religion." Jesus acknowledges other *true* paths and even lays out what makes a path *true*. Essentially, kindness.

If the path you're on isn't promoting kindness, or if you're seeing a lot of resulting negativity, or if you or someone else has been forcibly kidnapped and exorcised, it's important for you to understand that you aren't in a spiritually healthy environment.

Cleansing Prayer Notations

Before you perform a cleansing prayer, I'd like to share a few quick notes. The information below will help you choose the right prayer for your circumstances, and help you get in the right frame of mind for a successful cleansing.

Types of Cleansing Prayers

You'll find there are several different religious paths to choose from, including Christian, Jewish, Wiccan, and Native American. Though similar in design, each differ semantically according to the respected path and the number of people present for the cleansing. Before each path, there are quick recommendations regarding traditionally used incenses with that path. These are only suggestions, and as I noted previously, you are welcome to use any type or scent of incense available to you. Sage wands, sticks, cones, raw herbal incense, etc. are all fine. I don't believe the scent itself, or the distribution method of the smoke to be important. Rather, it's the presence of the scent within the smoke that is essential.

Pick your path, then decide which prayer best suits your situation. If you plan on performing the cleansing prayer alone, use the *Solo Version*. If you plan on having friends and family with you, you should use the *Group Version*.

If you're performing the cleansing prayer for someone else, at someone else's home, you should use the *Leader's Version*, which is suitable for *anyone* taking the lead to lend a helping hand to a suffering home, and so these are also appropriate for paranormal investigators, spiritual researchers, preachers, ministers, rabbis, priests, priestesses, and other spiritual leaders. For those using the Leader's Versions often, you might find an interest in my *Book of Cleansings* project, written specifically for these circumstances. With it, you gain distribution rights to freely copy the prayers and give them to clients and congregation members you wish to help.

Half of the prayers included are *House Cleansings*, and the other half are *Banishings*, which are cleansings that clean *everything*, even potentially good spirits. The *House Cleansings* leave wiggle room for deceased relatives to stick around. But...what if your passed relative is the one causing all the trouble? I'd recommend the Banishment version, used to include everything and everyone. If you choose to utilize the banishment, make sure it's absolutely necessary. Some paths, particularly Wiccan and Native American paths, frown on such practices unless it's truly needed. Both paths hold great reverence for their deceased ancestors, and a complete banishment should only be used if those ancestors are the ones causing the problems in the home, because they're going to get banished, whether they're guilty or not, if you use the banishment. I'm just saying, give this some thought. Of course, if there are frightened children in the mix, or you yourself are frightened, then, that trumps everything. You do what you've gotta do. No judgements here.

Parts of the Cleansing Prayers

There are three parts to the Cleansing Prayers. First, there is an *Opening Passage,* which sets the religious direction of the prayer. Next, there are four *Reiteration Passages*, which you repeat while walking through the home or property. You then complete the prayer with the final *Closing Passage*.

Techniques Vary

Some of my advice here goes against that of other folk's advice on cleansings, and you should know that there are *various* techniques for performing cleansings. Some may claim, *this* or *that* a vital aspect of the cleansings. Keep in mind that it's your faith, your force, and your convictions that will provide results. You don't need crucifixes, wands, circles, or red shoes on a Wednesday. You're dealing with the Spiritual, not physical, and ultimately, you must deal with it Spiritually. If someone says you *must* have a sage wand, but you only have sticks of lavender incense, it's okay to use the lavender. It's the presence of the smoke through the area that matters, not the particular scent, though some scents are traditional to certain religions. As you read through the various cleansing prayers, you'll note that I recommend certain herbs. These are just suggestions based on traditional uses of that herb within a particular religion, so you've got flexibility there. There are no mystical goose chases here.

Others might suggest that you open all the doors and windows during the cleansing, and you can't because you have pets and small children, it's okay. I personally believe that whatever binds a spirit to our world goes beyond the confines of doors and walls. These rules and restrictions only serve to cause doubt, and it's important that you understand these physical things you do during the cleansing aren't a smidgen as important as your faith and your conviction to send these spirits to the Light.

No Children
Children should not be present during the cleansing, as it may frighten and confuse them. It's important that children in the home be made to feel safe, above all else, and that means leaving them out of the cleansing.

Get Comfortable
Try to be comfortable during the cleansing. Some people prefer to perform the cleansing alone, so that they are less distracted, or less inhibited when they raise their voice to speak. Others may feel more comfortable with their friends and family around. Hauntings and cleansings can be frightening, and so some will feel more comfortable if they have supportive people by their side. Whatever makes you most comfortable is key.

Be Forceful, But Not Angry
Be forceful in your thoughts and words during the cleansing. Project your thoughts and words like you mean them, but don't let yourself become angry, or enraged. Be firm, but kind, and act from love, not anger. You may want to read over the prayer beforehand and familiarize yourself with its words and its intent before you begin, so you can speak with confidence during the prayer.

Stay Calm
Cleansings can be emotional. It's important to try and stay calm and in control. It's not uncommon though, for people to feel dizzy, light-headed, overheated, or anxious during a cleansing. If at any time you feel uncomfortable or unsteady, sit down and finish when you can. There are no time restraints on a

cleansing, and the important thing is that you don't faint or hurt yourself. If you need to sit through the entire prayer, that's fine, too. The smoke from the incense will eventually make its way to other rooms.

Have Faith

Before you begin, you need to genuinely believe that the cleansing will work. It's a common belief that spirits feed off our emotions and doubts, and I believe this to be true. Our doubts and lack of faith can serve as anchors for the spirits to remain in our world. Only your strength, and your faith, and your trust will make the cleansing successful.

Post-Cleansing Activity

Some spirits are more stubborn than others. It might take several cleansings over time to expel the most determined to stay, but I believe with each cleansing their hold to the material world is weakened, and they will eventually be expelled. Faith and patience are key, here.

Experiencing small amounts of activity after a cleansing is normal, too, particularly if there are deceased loved ones watching over the home. The cleansing itself can stir up other spirits as you push out the negative entities. Any remaining loved ones might be left anxious to let you know that they're still around.

Lingering Negativity

If you still feel a negative presence after the cleansing, that's normal, too. It can take several cleansings to truly rid a place of negativity. Some spirits are stronger, or more stubborn than others. Recite the cleansing prayer anytime you feel threatened or frightened, and slowly but surely, the

negative activity will eventually dwindle down.
Blessings to You

I hope that my words here have given you comfort, and you know that peace is possible. Even in the most frightening of circumstances, you can prevail, and you can take charge of your home. I wish you the best of luck, and may God Bless you and your home.

Christian Cleansing Prayers

Though any scent will work, I'd recommend Frankincense or Myrrh for those who desire a traditional scent while performing any of the following cleansing prayers.

Christian House Cleansing Prayer
Solo Version

(Light the incense and recite the opening passage below as you walk through the area.)

(Opening Passage)

My Heavenly Father, may your name be honored as I ask for your protection. Shield me from evil as I work to cleanse my home of negative spirits. Guide them, Almighty Lord, to your Heavenly light. Call to them, Lord, as I work to push them out and away from my home. Embrace them with your love, Lord, so they can know peace through your grace.

(Repeat the following four Reiteration Passages as needed, until you finish walking through the entire home.)

(Reiteration Passages)

I burn this incense to banish negativity. As it burns, its scent shall make known to the malevolent, that you are not welcome here. My Heavenly Father calls to you. The Light beckons you. This place is closing to you, and you will stay here no more.

I cleanse this area of all negativity, and all unwelcome spirits must leave. Only the angels looking after my home are welcome here. In God's name, and in Jesus' name, I pray that you see the Light.

All unwelcome beings in this home must leave. There will be no more negativity. You will leave my home alone, and you will leave my family in peace.

You will, in the name of God, go peacefully to the Light that calls you. You must go. This is not your home. God is calling you, and you must go to Him. All unwelcome spirits must leave.

(Closing Passage)

Heavenly Father, watch over all those who enter my home, whether in life, or in death, and show them your love. I thank you, Lord, for Blessing my home today with your grace and love. I pray that you keep my home safe.

May Your kingdom come, and Your Will be done here on Earth, as it is in Heaven.

Amen.

Christian House Cleansing Prayer
Group Version

(Light the incense and recite the opening passage below as you walk through the area.)

(Opening Passage)

Our Heavenly Father, may your name be honored as we ask for your protection. Shield us from evil as we work to cleanse our home of negative spirits. Guide them, Almighty Lord, to your Heavenly light. Call to these spirits, Lord, as we pray to push them out and away from our home. Embrace them with your love, Lord, so they can know peace through your grace.

(Repeat the following four Reiteration Passages as needed, until you finish walking through the entire home.)

(Reiteration Passages)

We burn this incense to banish negativity. As it burns, its scent shall make known to the malevolent, that you are not welcome here. Our Heavenly Father calls to you. The Light beckons you. This place is closing to you, and you will stay here no more.

We cleanse this area of all negativity, and all unwelcome spirits must leave. Only the angels looking after my home are welcome here. In God's name, and in Jesus' name, we pray that you see the Light.

All unwelcome beings in this home must leave. There will be no more negativity. You will leave our home alone, and you will leave our family in peace.

You will, in the name of God, go peacefully to the Light that calls you. You must go. This is not your home. God is calling you, and you must go to Him. All unwelcome spirits must leave.

(Closing Passage)

Heavenly Father, watch over all those who enter our home, whether in life, or in death, and show them your love. We thank you, Lord, for Blessing our home today with your grace and love. I pray that you keep our home and our family safe.

May Your kingdom come, and Your Will be done here on Earth, as it is in Heaven.

Amen.

Christian House Cleansing Prayer
Leader's Version

(Light the incense and recite the opening passage below as you walk through the area.)

(Opening Passage)

Our Heavenly Father, may your name be honored as we ask for your protection over those gathered here today. Shield us from evil as we work to cleanse this home of negative spirits. Guide them, Almighty Lord, to your Heavenly light. Call to them, Lord, as we work to push them out and away from this home. Embrace them with your love, Lord, so they can know peace through your grace.

(Repeat the following four Reiteration Passages as needed, until you finish walking through the entire home.)

(Reiteration Passages)

I burn this incense to banish negativity. As it burns, its scent shall make known to the malevolent, that you are not welcome here. Our Heavenly Father calls to you. The Light beckons you. This place is closing to you, and you will stay here no more.

I cleanse this area of all negativity, and all unwelcome spirits must leave. Only the angels looking after this home are welcome here. In God's name, and in Jesus' name, we pray that you see the Light.

All unwelcome beings in this home must leave. There will be no more negativity. You will leave this home alone, and you will leave this family in peace.

You will, in the name of God, go peacefully to the Light that calls you. You must go. This is not your home. God is calling you, and you must go to Him. All unwelcome spirits must leave.

(Closing Passage)

Heavenly Father, watch over all those who enter this home, whether in life, or in death, and show them your love. We thank you, Lord, for Blessing this home today with your grace and love. We pray that you keep this home safe.

May Your kingdom come, and Your Will be done here on Earth, as it is in Heaven.

Amen.

Christian Banishing
Solo Version

(Light the incense and recite the opening passage below as you walk through the area.)

(Opening Passage)

Our Heavenly Father, may your name be honored as I ask for your protection. Shield me from evil as I work to cleanse my home of spirits. Guide these spirits, Almighty Lord, to your Heavenly light. Call to them, Lord, as I work to push them out and away from my home. Embrace them with your love, Lord, so they can know peace through your grace.

(Repeat the following four Reiteration Passages as needed, until you finish walking through the entire home.)

(Reiteration Passages)

I burn this incense to banish negativity and all spirits. As it burns, its scent shall make known to the malevolent, that you are not welcome here. Our Heavenly Father calls to you. The Light beckons you. This place is closing to you, and you will stay here no more.

I cleanse this area of all negativity, and all unwelcome spirits must leave. In God's name, and in Jesus' name, I pray that you see the Light.

All spirits in this home must leave. There will be no more negativity. You will leave my home alone, and you will leave my family in peace.

You will, in the name of God, go peacefully to the Light that calls you. You must go. This is not your home. God is calling you, and you must go to Him. All spirits must leave.

(Closing Passage)

Heavenly Father, watch over all those who enter my home, whether in life, or in death, and show them your love. I thank you, Lord, for Blessing my home today with your grace and love. I pray that you keep my home safe. May Your kingdom come, and Your Will be done here on Earth, as it is in Heaven.

Amen.

Christian Banishing
Group Version

(Light the incense and recite the opening passage below as you walk through the area.)

(Opening Passage)

Our Heavenly Father, may your name be honored as we ask for your protection. Shield me us evil as we work to cleanse our home of spirits. Guide these spirits, Almighty Lord, to your Heavenly light. Call to them, Lord, as we work to push them out and away from our home. Embrace them with your love, Lord, so they can know peace through your grace.

(Repeat the following four Reiteration Passages as needed, until you finish walking through the entire home.)

(Reiteration Passages)

We burn this incense to banish negativity and all spirits. As it burns, its scent shall make known to the malevolent, that you are not welcome here. Our Heavenly Father calls to you. The Light beckons you. This place is closing to you, and you will stay here no more.

We cleanse this area of all negativity, and all unwelcome spirits must leave. In God's name, and in Jesus' name, we pray that you see the Light.

All spirits in this home must leave. There will be no more negativity. You will leave our home alone, and you will leave our family in peace.

You will, in the name of God, go peacefully to the Light that calls you. You must go. This is not your home. God is calling you, and you must go to Him. All spirits must leave.

(Closing Passage)

Heavenly Father, watch over all those who enter our home, whether in life, or in death, and show them your love. We thank you, Lord, for Blessing our home today with your grace and love. We pray that you keep our home safe. May Your kingdom come, and Your Will be done here on Earth, as it is in Heaven.

Amen.

Christian Banishing
Leader's Version

(Light the incense and recite the opening passage below as you walk through the area.)

(Opening Passage)

Our Heavenly Father, may your name be honored as we ask for your protection over each of us gathered here today. Shield us from evil as we work to cleanse this home of negative spirits. Guide these spirits, Almighty Lord, to your Heavenly light. Call to them, Lord, as we work to push them out and away from this home. Embrace them with your love, Lord, so they can know peace through your grace.

(Repeat the following four Reiteration Passages as needed, until you finish walking through the entire home.)

(Reiteration Passages)

I burn this incense to banish negativity. As it burns, its scent shall make known to the malevolent, that you are not welcome here. Our Heavenly Father calls to you. The Light beckons you. This place is closing to you, and you will stay here no more.

I cleanse this area of all negativity, and all spirits must leave. In God's name, and in Jesus' name, we pray that you see the Light.

All spirits in this home must leave. There will be no more negativity. You will leave this home alone, and you will leave this family in peace.

You will, in the name of God, go peacefully to the Light that calls you. You must go. This is not your home. God is calling you, and you must go to Him. All spirits must leave.

(Closing Passage)

Heavenly Father, watch over all those who enter this home, whether in life, or in death, and show them your love. We thank you, Lord, for Blessing this home today with your grace and love. We pray that you keep this home safe.

May Your kingdom come, and Your Will be done here on Earth, as it is in Heaven.

Amen.

Jewish Cleansing Prayers

    I'd recommend Frankincense or Myrrh for those who desire a traditional scent. Both are widely available and smell beautiful enough to linger through the home for a few days.

Jewish House Cleansing Prayer
Solo Version

(Light the incense and recite the opening passage below as you walk through the area.)

(Opening Passage)

Lord, God, I ask for your protection as I work to cleanse my home of negativity. Shield me from evil, Lord, as I work to cleanse my home of negative spirits. Guide them, Almighty Lord. Call to them, as I work to push them out and away from my home. Embrace them with your love, Lord, so they can know peace through your grace.

(While the previous passage is directed at our Lord, the following passages are directed toward the spirit/s. Repeat the following four Reiteration Passages as needed, until you finish walking through the entire home.)

(Reiteration Passages)

I burn this incense to banish negativity. As it burns, its scent shall make known to the malevolent, that you are not welcome here. Our Lord calls to you. The Light beckons you. This place is closing to you, and you will stay here no more.

I cleanse this area of all negativity, and all unwelcome spirits must leave. Only the angels looking after my home are welcome here. In God's name, I pray that you see the Light.

All unwelcome beings in this home must leave. There will be no more negativity. You will leave my home alone, and you will leave my family in peace.

You will, in the name of God, go peacefully to the Light that calls you. You must go. This is not your home. God is calling you, and you must go to Him. All unwelcome spirits must leave.

(Closing Passage)

My Lord, watch over all those who enter my home, whether in life, or in death, and show them your love. Blessed is He who is the master of both worlds, and the Lord of peace. Show them your peace.

Through my words, I serve you Lord, with the whole of my heart, and I thank you for Blessing my home today with your grace and love.

Jewish House Cleansing Prayer
Group Version

(Light the incense and recite the opening passage below as you walk through the area.)

(Opening Passage)

Lord, God, we ask for your protection as we work to cleanse our home of negativity. Shield us from evil, Lord, as we work to cleanse our home of negative spirits. Guide them, Almighty Lord. Call to them, as I work to push them out and away from my home. Embrace them with your love, Lord, so they can know peace through your grace.

(Repeat the following four Reiteration Passages as needed, until you finish walking through the entire home.)

(Reiteration Passages)

We burn this incense to banish negativity. As it burns, its scent shall make known to the malevolent, that you are not welcome here. Our Lord calls to you. The Light beckons you. This place is closing to you, and you will stay here no more.

We cleanse this area of all negativity, and all unwelcome spirits must leave. Only the angels looking after our home are welcome here. In God's name, we pray that you see the Light.

All unwelcome beings in our home must leave. There will be no more negativity. You will leave our home alone, and you will leave our family in peace.

You will, in the name of God, go peacefully to the Light that calls you. You must go. This is not your home. God is calling you, and you must go to Him. All unwelcome spirits must leave.

(Closing Passage)

My Lord, watch over all those who enter our home, whether in life, or in death, and show them your love. Blessed is He who is the master of both worlds, and the Lord of peace. Show them your peace.

Through our prayers we serve you Lord, with the whole of our hearts, and we thank you for Blessing our home today with your grace and love.

Jewish House Cleansing Prayer
Leader's Version

(Light the incense and recite the opening passage below as you walk through the area.)

(Opening Passage)

Lord, God, we ask for your protection over those gathered here today, as we work to cleanse this home of negativity. Shield us from evil, Lord, as we work to cleanse this home of negative spirits. Guide them, Almighty Lord. Call to them, as we work to push them out and away from this home. Embrace them with your love, Lord, so they can know peace through your grace.

(Repeat the following four Reiteration Passages as needed, until you finish walking through the entire home.)

(Reiteration Passages)

We burn this incense to banish negativity. As it burns, its scent shall make known to the malevolent, that you are not welcome here. Our Lord calls to you. The Light beckons you. This place is closing to you, and you will stay here no more.

We cleanse this area of all negativity, and all unwelcome spirits must leave. Only the angels looking after this home are welcome here. In God's name, we pray that you see the Light.

All unwelcome beings in this home must leave. There will be no more negativity. You will leave this home alone, and you will leave this family in peace.

You will, in the name of God, go peacefully to the Light that calls you. You must go. This is not your home. God is calling you, and you must go to Him. All unwelcome spirits must leave.

(Closing Passage)

Our Lord, watch over all those who enter this home, whether in life, or in death, and show them your love. Blessed is He who is the master of both worlds, and the Lord of peace. Show them your peace.

Through our prayers, we serve you Lord, with the whole of our hearts, and we thank you for Blessing this home today with your grace and love.

Jewish Banishing
Solo Version

(Light the incense and recite the opening passage below as you walk through the area.)

(Opening Passage)

Lord, God, I ask for your protection as I work to cleanse my home of negativity. Shield me from evil, Lord, as I work to cleanse my home of spirits. Guide them, Almighty Lord. Call to them, as I work to push them out and away from my home. Embrace them with your love, Lord, so they can know peace through your grace.

(Repeat the following four Reiteration Passages as needed, until you finish walking through the entire home.)

(Reiteration Passages)

I burn this incense to banish negativity. As it burns, its scent shall make known to the malevolent, that you are not welcome here. My Lord calls to you. The Light beckons you. This place is closing to you, and you will stay here no more.

I cleanse this area of all negativity, and all spirits must leave. In God's name, I pray that you see the Light.

All unwelcome beings in this home must leave. There will be no more negativity. You will leave my home alone, and you will leave my family in peace.

You will, in the name of God, go peacefully to the Light that calls you. You must go. This is not your home. God is calling you, and you must go to Him. All spirits must leave.

(Closing Passage)

My Lord, watch over all those who enter my home, whether in life, or in death, and show them your love. Blessed is He who is the master of both worlds, and the Lord of peace. Show them your peace.

Through my prayer, I serve you Lord, with the whole of my heart, and I thank you for Blessing my home today with your grace and love.

Jewish Banishing
Group Version

(Light the incense and recite the opening passage below as you walk through the area.)

(Opening Passage)

Lord, God, we ask for your protection as we work to cleanse our home of negativity. Shield us from evil, Lord, as we work to cleanse our home of spirits. Guide them, Almighty Lord. Call to them, as I work to push them out and away from my home. Embrace them with your love, Lord, so they can know peace through your grace.

(Repeat the following four Reiteration Passages as needed, until you finish walking through the entire home.)

(Reiteration Passages)

We burn this incense to banish negativity. As it burns, its scent shall make known to the malevolent, that you are not welcome here. Our Lord calls to you. The Light beckons you. This place is closing to you, and you will stay here no more.

We cleanse this area of all negativity, and all spirits must leave. In God's name, we pray that you see the Light.

All unwelcome beings in our home must leave. There will be no more negativity. You will leave our home alone, and you will leave our family in peace.

You will, in the name of God, go peacefully to the Light that calls you. You must go. This is not your home. God is calling you, and you must go to Him. All spirits must leave.

(Closing Passage)

My Lord, watch over all those who enter our home, whether in life, or in death, and show them your love. Blessed is He who is the master of both worlds, and the Lord of peace. Show them your peace.

Through our prayers, we serve you Lord, with the whole of our hearts, and we thank you for Blessing our home today with your grace and love.

Jewish Banishing
Leader's Version

(Light the incense and recite the opening passage below as you walk through the area.)

(Opening Passage)

Lord, God, we ask for your protection over those gathered here today, as we work to cleanse this home of negativity. Shield us from evil, Lord, as we work to cleanse this home of spirits. Guide them, Almighty Lord. Call to them, as we work to push them out and away from this home. Embrace them with your love, Lord, so they can know peace through your grace.

(Repeat the following four Reiteration Passages as needed, until you finish walking through the entire home.)

(Reiteration Passages)

We burn this incense to banish negativity. As it burns, its scent shall make known to the malevolent, that you are not welcome here. Our Lord calls to you. The Light beckons you. This place is closing to you, and you will stay here no more.

We cleanse this area of all negativity, and all spirits must leave. In God's name, we pray that you see the Light.

All unwelcome beings in this home must leave. There will be no more negativity. You will leave this home alone, and you will leave this family in peace.

You will, in the name of God, go peacefully to the Light that calls you. You must go. This is not your home. God is calling you, and you must go to Him. All spirits must leave.

(Closing Passage)

My Lord, watch over all those who enter this home, whether in life, or in death, and show them your love. Blessed is He who is the master of both worlds, and the Lord of peace. Show them your peace.

Through our prayers, we I serve you Lord, with the whole of our hearts, and we thank you for Blessing this home today with your grace and love.

Wiccan Cleansing Prayers

Traditional Wiccan incenses include rosemary, lavender, frankincense, myrrh, oakmoss, rose, and *many* other aromatic European herbs, though modern practitioners are known to use a variety of plants from around the world as they absorb practices from other pagan cultures. It's not uncommon for Wiccans to use sage sticks, though it's a practice originally indigenous to the natives of the Americas. These modern adaptions illustrate the leniency you have here, so feel free to pick a scent you'll enjoy having around for a day or two.

Wiccan House Cleansing Prayer
Solo Version

(Light the incense and recite the opening passage below as you walk through the area.)

(Opening Passage)

My Lord and Lady, I ask for your protection today. Shield me, my God and Goddess, and protect me from evil as I work to cleanse my home of negative spirits. Guide them to Your light. Call to them as I work to push them out and away from my home. Embrace them with your strength, my Lord. Embrace them with your love, my Lady. May they see your light and your truth, and come to peace through your graces.

(Repeat the following four Reiteration Passages as needed, until you finish walking through the entire home.)

(Reiteration Passages)

I burn this incense to banish negativity. As it burns, its scent shall make known to the malevolent, that you are not welcome here. The Lord and Lady call to you. The Light beckons you. This place is closing to you, and you will stay here no more.

I cleanse this area of all negativity, and all unwelcome spirits must leave. Only the angels looking after my home are welcome here. I pray that you see the Light that shines for you, from our Mother and Father. They are calling you to the light.

All unwelcome beings in my home must leave. There will be no more negativity. You will leave my home alone, and you will leave my family in peace.

You will, in the name of our Father and Mother, go peacefully to the Light that calls you. You must go. This is not your home. They are calling you, and you must go to Them. All unwelcome spirits must leave.

(Closing Passage)

My Lord and Lady, my Mother and Father, my God and Goddess, watch over all those who enter my home, whether in life, or in death, and show them your love. I thank you for Blessing my home today with your grace and your love. I pray that you keep me and my home safe.

So mote it be.

Wiccan House Cleansing Prayer
Group Version

(Light the incense and recite the opening passage below as you walk through the area.)

(Opening Passage)

Our Lord and Lady, we ask for your protection today, as we gather to cleanse our home of negativity. Shield us, our God and Goddess, and protect us from evil as we work to cleanse our home of negative spirits. Guide them to Your light. Call to them as we work to push them out and away from our home. Embrace them with your strength, our Lord. Embrace them with your love, our Lady. May they see your light and your truth, and come to peace through your graces.

(Repeat the following four Reiteration Passages as needed, until you finish walking through the entire home.)

(Reiteration Passages)

We burn this incense to banish negativity. As it burns, its scent shall make known to the malevolent, that you are not welcome here.

The Lord and Lady call to you. The Light beckons you. This place is closing to you, and you will stay here no more.

We cleanse this area of all negativity, and all unwelcome spirits must leave. Only the angels looking after our home are welcome here. We pray that you see the Light that shines for you, from our Mother and Father. They are calling you to the light.

All unwelcome beings in our home must leave. There will be no more negativity. You will leave our home alone, and you will leave our family in peace.

You will, in the name of our Father and our Mother, go peacefully to the Light that calls you. They are calling you, and you must go to Them. All unwelcome spirits must leave.

(Closing Passage)

Our Lord and Lady, our Mother and Father, our God and Goddess, watch over all those who enter our home, whether in life, or in death, and show them your love. We thank you for Blessing our home today with your grace and your love. We pray that you keep us safe. So mote it be.

Wiccan House Cleansing Prayer
Leader's Version

(Light the incense and recite the opening passage below as you walk through the area.)

(Opening Passage)

Our Lord and Lady, we ask for your protection today, as we gather to cleanse this home of negativity. Shield us, our God and Goddess, and protect us from evil as we work to cleanse this home of negative spirits. Guide them to Your light. Call to them as we work to push them out and away from this home. Embrace them with your strength, our Lord. Embrace them with your love, our Lady. May they see your light and your truth, and come to peace through your graces.

(Repeat the following four Reiteration Passages as needed, until you finish walking through the entire home.)

(Reiteration Passages)

We burn this incense to banish negativity. As it burns, its scent shall make known to the malevolent, that you are not welcome here.

The Lord and Lady call to you. The Light beckons you. This place is closing to you, and you will stay here no more.

We cleanse this area of all negativity, and all unwelcome spirits must leave. Only the angels looking after this home are welcome here. We pray that you see the Light that shines for you, from our Mother and Father. They are calling you to the light.

All unwelcome beings in this home must leave. There will be no more negativity. You will leave this home alone, and you will leave this family in peace.

You will, in the name of our Father and our Mother, go peacefully to the Light that calls you. They are calling you, and you must go to Them. All unwelcome spirits must leave.

(Closing Passage)

Our Lord and Lady, our Mother and Father, our God and Goddess, watch over all those who enter this home, whether in life, or in death, and show them your love. We thank you for Blessing this home today with your grace and your love. We pray that you keep us safe. So mote it be.

Wiccan Banishing
Solo Version

(Light the incense and recite the opening passage below as you walk through the area.)

(Opening Passage)

My Lord and Lady, I ask for your protection today. Shield me, my God and Goddess, and protect me from evil as I work to cleanse my home of spirits. Guide them to Your light. Call to them as I work to push them out and away from my home. Embrace them with your strength, my Lord. Embrace them with your love, my Lady. May they see your light and your truth, and come to peace through your graces.

(Repeat the following four Reiteration Passages as needed, until you finish walking through the entire home.)

(Reiteration Passages)

I burn this incense to banish negativity. As it burns, its scent shall make known to the malevolent, that you are not welcome here. The Lord and Lady call to you. The Light beckons you. This place is closing to you, and you will stay here no more.

I cleanse this area of all negativity, and all spirits must leave. I pray that you see the Light that shines for you, from our Mother and Father. They are calling you to the light.

All unwelcome beings in my home must leave. There will be no more negativity. You will leave my home alone, and you will leave my family in peace.

You will, in the name of our Father and Mother, go peacefully to the Light that calls you. You must go. This is not your home. They are calling you, and you must go to Them. All spirits must leave.

(Closing Passage)

My Lord and Lady, my Mother and Father, my God and Goddess, watch over all those who enter my home, whether in life, or in death, and show them your love. I thank you for Blessing my home today with your grace and your love. I pray that you keep me and my home safe.

So mote it be.

Wiccan Banishing
Group Version

(Light the incense and recite the opening passage below as you walk through the area.)

(Opening Passage)

Our Lord and Lady, we ask for your protection today, as we gather to cleanse our home of negativity. Shield us, our God and Goddess, and protect us from evil as we work to cleanse our home of negative spirits. Guide them to Your light. Call to them as we work to push them out and away from our home. Embrace them with your strength, our Lord. Embrace them with your love, our Lady. May they see your light and your truth, and come to peace through your graces.

(Repeat the following four Reiteration Passages as needed, until you finish walking through the entire home.)

(Reiteration Passages)

We burn this incense to banish negativity. As it burns, its scent shall make known to the malevolent, that you are not welcome here.

The Lord and Lady call to you. The Light beckons you. This place is closing to you, and you will stay here no more.

We cleanse this area of all negativity, and all spirits must leave. We pray that you see the Light that shines for you, from our Mother and Father. They are calling you to the light.

All unwelcome beings in our home must leave. There will be no more negativity. You will leave our home alone, and you will leave our family in peace.

You will, in the name of our Father and our Mother, go peacefully to the Light that calls you. They are calling you, and you must go to Them. All spirits must leave.

(Closing Passage)

Our Lord and Lady, our Mother and Father, our God and Goddess, watch over all those who enter our home, whether in life, or in death, and show them your love. I thank you for Blessing our home today with your grace and your love. We pray that you keep us safe.

So mote it be.

Wiccan Banishing
Leader's Version

(Light the incense and recite the opening passage below as you walk through the area.)

(Opening Passage)

Our Lord and Lady, we ask for your protection today, as we gather to cleanse this home of negativity. Shield us, our God and Goddess, and protect us from evil as we work to cleanse this home of negative spirits. Guide them to Your light. Call to them as we work to push them out and away from this home. Embrace them with your strength, our Lord. Embrace them with your love, our Lady. May they see your light and your truth, and come to peace through your graces.

(Repeat the following four Reiteration Passages as needed, until you finish walking through the entire home.)

(Reiteration Passages)

We burn this incense to banish negativity. As it burns, its scent shall make known to the malevolent, that you are not welcome here.

The Lord and Lady call to you. The Light beckons you. This place is closing to you, and you will stay here no more.

We cleanse this area of all negativity, and all spirits must leave. We pray that you see the Light that shines for you, from our Mother and Father. They are calling you to the light.

All unwelcome beings in this home must leave. There will be no more negativity. You will leave this home alone, and you will leave this family in peace.

You will, in the name of our Father and our Mother, go peacefully to the Light that calls you. They are calling you, and you must go to Them. All spirits must leave.

(Closing Passage)

Our Lord and Lady, our Mother and Father, our God and Goddess, watch over all those who enter this home, whether in life, or in death, and show them your love. We thank you for Blessing this home today with your grace and your love. We pray that you keep us safe.

So mote it be.

Native American Prayers

The following are suggested prayers for those that follow a path influenced by any of the major Native American Tribes. These prayers capture the essence of the various tribes and are suitable if there isn't a spiritual leader available to perform a traditional cleansing from an officially recognized tribe. These aren't sanctioned by any of the tribes, but they were written with great respect and reverence for each of them.

These prayers are generic and are appropriate for any of the tribes, or a mix of several. If you're like me, a direct descendent from ancestors of several different nations, then you'll find these prayers accommodate your rich heritage and seek to honor each of these American tribes.

The recommended incenses for use during these Native American based prayers, also called Smudging, include sage sticks, copal, cedar, pine, oakmoss, rose, and even tobacco. Some practitioners use feathers, often from an eagle or other large bird, to fan the smoke of the incense as it burns.

Modern practitioners have incorporated non-indigenous herbs from Europe in with the traditional herbs, for blends such as sage and lavender, or sage and rosemary, which illustrates that there are no hard-fast rules when it comes to incense and the particular scent you choose. So, choose a scent you'll find pleasant.

Native American Cleansing Prayer
Solo Version

(Light the incense and recite the opening passage below as you walk through the area.)

(Opening Passage)

Hear me, Great Spirit, as I call to you for help and protection. Shield me from evil as I work to cleanse my home of negative ghosts. Guide them to you, Great Spirit, for they are lost and can't stay here. Call to these lost souls, Great Spirit, as I pray to push them out and away from my home. Embrace them with your light, Great Spirit, and show them their path home.

(Repeat the following four Reiteration Passages as needed, until you finish walking through the entire home.)

(Reiteration Passages)

I burn this incense to banish negativity. As it burns, its scent shall make known to the malevolent, that you are not welcome here. The Great Spirit calls to you. The Light beckons you. This place is closing to you, and you will stay here no more.

I cleanse this area of all negativity, and all unwelcome spirits must leave. Only the ancestors looking after my home are welcome here. I pray that you see the Light.

All unwelcome beings in my home must leave. There will be no more negativity. You will leave my home alone, and you will leave my home in peace.

You will go peacefully to the Light that calls you. You must go. This is not your home. The Great Spirit is calling you, and you must go. All unwelcome ghosts must leave.

(Closing Passage)

Great Spirit, watch over all those who enter my home, whether in life, or in death, and show them your love. I thank you, Great Spirit, for Blessing our home today with your grace and love. I pray that you keep my home and my family safe.

Thank you, Great Spirit.

Native American Cleansing Prayer
Group Version

(Light the incense and recite the opening passage below as you walk through the area.)

(Opening Passage)

Hear our prayers, Great Spirit, as we call to you for help and protection. Shield us from evil as we work to cleanse our home of negative ghosts. Guide them to you, Great Spirit, for they are lost and can't stay here. Call to these lost souls, Great Spirit, as we pray to push them out and away from our home. Embrace them with your light, Great Spirit, and show them their path home.

(Repeat the following four Reiteration Passages as needed, until you finish walking through the entire home.)

(Reiteration Passages)

We burn this incense to banish negativity. As it burns, its scent shall make known to the malevolent, that you are not welcome here. The Great Spirit calls to you. The Light beckons you. This place is closing to you, and you will stay here no more.

We cleanse this area of all negativity, and all unwelcome spirits must leave. Only the ancestors looking after our home are welcome here. We pray that you see the Light.

All unwelcome beings in our home must leave. There will be no more negativity. You will leave our home alone, and you will leave our home in peace.

You will go peacefully to the Light that calls you. You must go. This is not your home. The Great Spirit is calling you, and you must go. All unwelcome ghosts must leave.

(Closing Passage)

Great Spirit, watch over all those who enter our home, whether in life, or in death, and show them your love. We thank you, Great Spirit, for Blessing our home today with your grace and love. We pray that you keep our home and our family safe.

Thank you, Great Spirit.

Native American Cleansing Prayer
Leader's Version

(Light the incense and recite the opening passage below as you walk through the area.)

(Opening Passage)

Hear our prayers, Great Spirit, as we call to you for help and protection. Shield us from evil as we work to cleanse this home of negative ghosts. Guide them to you, Great Spirit, for they are lost and can't stay here. Call to these lost souls, Great Spirit, as we pray to push them out and away from this home. Embrace them with your light, Great Spirit, and show them their path home.

(Repeat the following four Reiteration Passages as needed, until you finish walking through the entire home.)

(Reiteration Passages)

We burn this incense to banish negativity. As it burns, its scent shall make known to the malevolent, that you are not welcome here. The Great Spirit calls to you. The Light beckons you. This place is closing to you, and you will stay here no more.

We cleanse this area of all negativity, and all unwelcome spirits must leave. Only the ancestors looking after this home and this family are welcome here. We pray that you see the Light.

All unwelcome beings in this home must leave. There will be no more negativity. You will leave this home alone, and you will leave our home in peace.

You will go peacefully to the Light that calls you. You must go. This is not your home. The Great Spirit is calling you, and you must go. All unwelcome ghosts must leave.

(Closing Passage)

Great Spirit, watch over all those who enter this home, whether in life, or in death, and show them your love. We thank you, Great Spirit, for Blessing this home today with your grace and love. We pray that you keep this home and this family safe.

Thank you, Great Spirit.

Native American Banishing
Solo Version

(Light the incense and recite the opening passage below as you walk through the area.)

(Opening Passage)

Hear me, Great Spirit, as I call to you for help and protection. Shield me from evil as I work to cleanse my home of negative ghosts. Guide them to you, Great Spirit, for they are lost and can't stay here. Call to these lost souls, Great Spirit, as I pray to push them out and away from my home. Embrace them with your light, Great Spirit, and show them their path home.

(Repeat the following four Reiteration Passages as needed, until you finish walking through the entire home.)

(Reiteration Passages)

I burn this incense to banish negativity. As it burns, its scent shall make known to the malevolent, that you are not welcome here. The Great Spirit calls to you. The Light beckons you. This place is closing to you, and you will stay here no more.

I cleanse this area of all negativity, and all spirits must leave. I pray that you see the Light.

All ghosts in my home must leave. There will be no more negativity. You will leave my home alone, and you will leave my home in peace.

You will go peacefully to the Light that calls you. You must go. This is not your home. The Great Spirit is calling you, and you must go. All ghosts must leave.

(Closing Passage)

Great Spirit, watch over all those who enter my home, whether in life, or in death, and show them your love. I thank you, Great Spirit, for Blessing our home today with your grace and love. I pray that you keep my home and my family safe.

Thank you, Great Spirit.

Native American Banishing
Group Version

(Light the incense and recite the opening passage below as you walk through the area.)

(Opening Passage)

Hear our prayers, Great Spirit, as we call to you for help and protection. Shield us from evil as we work to cleanse our home of ghosts. Guide them to you, Great Spirit, for they are lost and can't stay here. Call to these lost souls, Great Spirit, as we pray to push them out and away from our home. Embrace them with your light, Great Spirit, and show them their path home.

(Repeat the following four Reiteration Passages as needed, until you finish walking through the entire home.)

(Reiteration Passages)

We burn this incense to banish negativity. As it burns, its scent shall make known to the malevolent, that you are not welcome here. The Great Spirit calls to you. The Light beckons you. This place is closing to you, and you will stay here no more.

We cleanse this area of all negativity, and all ghosts leave. We pray that you see the Light.

All ghosts in our home must leave. There will be no more negativity. You will leave our home alone, and you will leave our home in peace.

You will go peacefully to the Light that calls you. You must go. This is not your home. The Great Spirit is calling you, and you must go. All ghosts must leave.

(Closing Passage)

Great Spirit, watch over all those who enter our home, whether in life, or in death, and show them your love. We thank you, Great Spirit, for Blessing our home today with your grace and love. We pray that you keep our home and our family safe.

Thank you, Great Spirit.

Native American Banishing
Leader's Version

(Light the incense and recite the opening passage below as you walk through the area.)

(Opening Passage)

Hear our prayers, Great Spirit, as we call to you for help and protection. Shield us from evil as we work to cleanse this home of ghosts. Guide them to you, Great Spirit, for they are lost and can't stay here. Call to these lost souls, Great Spirit, as we pray to push them out and away from this home. Embrace them with your light, Great Spirit, and show them their path home.

(Repeat the following four Reiteration Passages as needed, until you finish walking through the entire home.)

(Reiteration Passages)

We burn this incense to banish negativity. As it burns, its scent shall make known to the malevolent, that you are not welcome here. The Great Spirit calls to you. The Light beckons you. This place is closing to you, and you will stay here no more.

We cleanse this area of all negativity, and all ghosts must leave. We pray that you see the Light.

All ghosts in this home must leave. There will be no more negativity. You will leave this home alone, and you will leave our home in peace.

You will go peacefully to the Light that calls you. You must go. This is not your home. The Great Spirit is calling you, and you must go. All unwelcome ghosts must leave.

(Closing Passage)

Great Spirit, watch over all those who enter this home, whether in life, or in death, and show them your love. We thank you, Great Spirit, for Blessing this home today with your grace and love. We pray that you keep this home and this family safe.

Thank you, Great Spirit.

Thank you, dearest reader, for your interest in my work. It's my sincerest hope that my words have helped you get on the right path to finding peace in your home, and that this book brought a bit of light into the darkness.

I'd also like to thank the following people for sharing their time with me in the field, which ultimately, made this book possible: **Chad Hughes, Timothy Smith, William Altenreid, Timothy Stuckey, Timothy Lowman, Shawna Bowman, Charlie Everitt, Allison Maxwell, Scherrie Ashworth, and Andrea Ashworth.**

My affiliation with Lufkin Paranormal Investigators blessed me with many online acquaintances and friendships with other paranormal groups. Being a part of these online groups and friendships afforded me many insights regarding the inter-workings and concerns within other paranormal groups. These insights proved most helpful with organizing my thoughts for this book. I'd like to thank each of these groups, who not only proved helpful and friendly, but unknowingly served as a continuing source of inspiration for the material presented. If you're in their neck of the woods, and you find yourself looking for a group of investigators, you'd be hard pressed to find better folks than these.

Lufkin Paranormal Investigators based in East Texas.
Midnight Paranormal Society based in San Antonio, Texas.
Texas State Paranormal Society based in West Texas.
Elk Valley Paranormal based in Tennessee.
Kansas City Paranormal based in Kansas.
Greater Texas Paranormal based In San Marcus.
Twilight Shadows North Paranormal based in England.
Twin Cities Paranormal based in Minnesota.
Paranormal Society World based in the Netherlands.

Many thanks also, to **La Unica** restaurant in Lufkin, Texas, for allowing my LPI colleagues and I to research and investigate the property, which remains to this day, one of our most interesting cases. I'd like to thank the staff at the **Menger Hotel** in San Antonio, for their permission to investigate the grounds and their subsequent guidance around the property by staff on several occasions over the years. I'd also like to thank the **Texas Rangers** stationed in San Antonio for their generous insights, stories of colonial Texas, and their bone-chilling tales of odd night-watches. Also, out of San Antonio, I'd like to thank members of the **Daughters of the Republic** and the **Alamo Defenders Descendants Association** for their personal insights and walks through the Alamo chapel and grounds.

I'd also like to thank friends **Bob Sanders** and **Joan Fulton Headley** for their devotion to preserving Texas history. Though I've never met nor spoken with **Phil Collins,** I'd like to thank him, too, for his heartwarming work with the Alamo. As a descendent of a fallen Alamo fighter, I'd like to thank each of these three from the bottom of my heart, for helping keep their spirit and the spirit of Texas alive for all to remember. Bless you three.

Many thanks also to friends, **Sharon Fuller**, **Lianne Tate** and **Sharon Hughes**, for their invaluable friendship and feedback. A huge thanks to my husband, **James**, without whose support this book would not have been possible. Thanks also to my parents **Larry** and **Joyce Bowman**, my sister, **Shawna**, for their support, encouragement, and guidance in *everything*.

If you found my words helpful to you or your family, please consider leaving a kind review, so that others might know that help *is* available. I thank you again, dearest reader, and wish you the brightest of blessings.

Dedicated in Loving Memory to
BOB BOWMAN
(1936-2013)

My sweet uncle, Bob Bowman, was the most notable Texas historian of our generation and his contributions to the preservation and retelling of Texas history is unmatched by another. My uncle loved a good ghost story, too. He believed the ghosts of Texas to be as relevant to history as the battles, and he wrote several books on hauntings proving as much. Though our family misses him, he lives on through his work. Like the Alamo, a favorite subject of his, he will be remembered.

About Dawn Flowers

Author, Dawn Flowers, is an East Texas writer, born and raised under the shade of the Piney Woods where she resides with her family and pets. She released her first book in 2001 and has since authored and published over thirty books on a wide range of subjects, including both fiction and non-fiction works, under a variety of pen names.

Her non-fiction titles reflect her love of religions, while her non-fiction titles reflect her love of horror. Most noted for her non-fiction metaphysical titles, she's also written and compiled twelve children's books for kids of the Christian, Jewish, and Wiccan faiths. Seven of her works were written and compiled under the name of Dawn Nefer-Aten, and were published for a non-profit, live-action, role-playing group, Amtgard, during her citizenship within the Kingdom of the Wetlands.

Her first fiction project, a short story titled, *In the Forest*, appeared in an eponymously titled collaborative book project with four other East Texas writers in 2011. The story was later revised into a horror novella. She then went on to write a series of six horror stories for children, with several more in the works.

Her most notable non-fiction works include *The Book of Dark & Light Shadows* and *The Spell Book of Wiccan Shadows*. Both titles were released online in 2011, and both rose to reach Amazon's #1 Best Seller rank for their categories, including Mysticism, Witchcraft, Paganism, and Neo Paganism. Almost a decade later, both titles continue to teeter within Amazon's top 100 best-selling books within their categories.

For a complete list of available titles, bulk offers, or to keep up with new releases, you may visit **DawnaFlowers.com**, or follow her Facebook Page: ***Dawna Flowers Books.***

Children's Religions Titles
The Little Christian's Learning Series, (7 Book Set)
The Little Jewish Learning Set (2 Book Set)
The Little Wiccan's Set (Coming Back Soon)

Adult Religions & Spirituality Titles
The Book of Dark & Light Shadows
The Spell Book of Wiccan Shadows
The Wiccan Holiday Cookbook
Witch Wars
Help with Hauntings

Adult Fiction Titles
In the Forest, Horror Novella
Sea Loot, Horror Novel (Coming Soon!)
Neighbors, Horror Novel (Coming Soon!)

Childrens Fiction Titles
Along Came Cthulhu
Bigfoot of the Big Woods
Story of Krampus
Crazy 'Coon Lady
Wolves of Woodsmen County
Helpful Hank
Sally Scratch & the Squirrel (Coming soon!)
The Bat House Bag (Coming soon!)

Help with Hauntings:
A Guide to Cleansing your Home of Spirits and Ghosts
Copyright 2019 Dawna Flowers
Published by Under the Moon, an Independent Publishing House, owned by Dawna Flowers.
Distributed by Dawna Flowers and Amazon.

All rights reserved under international and Pan American Copyright Conventions.
No part of this book may be reproduced manually or electronically
without written permission from the author,
dawnaflowers@live.com

Published in the United States.
Manufactured in the United Sates.
First Edition, 2019.

ISBN-13: 9781792789014